It's Never Too Late to Be Worthy Of ...

A Guide to Discovering Your True Worth

Susan L. Zirilli

BALBOA
PRESS

A DIVISION OF HAY HOUSE

Scripture quotations marked NIV are taken from the Holy Bible, New International Version®. NIV®. Copyright © 1973, 1978, 1984 by International Bible Society. Used by permission of Zondervan. All rights reserved.

Balboa Press books may be ordered through booksellers or by contacting:

Balboa Press
A Division of Hay House
1663 Liberty Drive
Bloomington, IN 47403
www.balboapress.com
1 (877) 407-4847

Because of the dynamic nature of the Internet, any web addresses or links contained in this book may have changed since publication and may no longer be valid. The views expressed in this work are solely those of the author and do not necessarily reflect the views of the publisher, and the publisher hereby disclaims any responsibility for them.

The author of this book does not dispense medical advice or prescribe the use of any technique as a form of treatment for physical, emotional, or medical problems without the advice of a physician, either directly or indirectly. The intent of the author is only to offer information of a general nature to help you in your quest for emotional and spiritual well-being. In the event you use any of the information in this book for yourself, which is your constitutional right, the author and the publisher assume no responsibility for your actions.

Any people depicted in stock imagery provided by Thinkstock are models, and such images are being used for illustrative purposes only. Certain stock imagery © Thinkstock.

Print information available on the last page.

ISBN: 978-1-5043-7608-2 (sc)
ISBN: 978-1-5043-7609-9 (hc)
ISBN: 978-1-5043-7607-5 (e)

Library of Congress Control Number: 2017907302

Balboa Press rev. date: 07/31/2017

To all who never feel worthy enough or worthy at all,

all who always put everyone and everything before themselves,

all who need to move themselves higher on their own list,

and all who suffer from self-imposed unimportance.

Also to the wonderful, worthy people who serve as our role models in this process.

Contents

wor·thy

/ˈwərTHē/

adjective

1. deserving effort, attention, or respect.

Intention

Our time is now
- to begin the examination of our often less-than-clear consciences that, permit personal, self-inflicted injustice to occur so naturally, and
- to take back our "worth," rescuing it from our naïve neglect and bringing our value out into the light for all to see.

We are all born worthy. Our hearts remind us of this irrefutable truth as it seeks to reunite us with its precious light.

Our time has come
- to awaken our worthiness with confidence and expectancy.
- to speak up, speak out, and speak the truths of how valuable and glorious we are by composing an evolved narrative.

Because we matter.

Because we deserve more.

Once worthiness is a part of your life formula, there is no mountain you can't climb, no dragon you can't slay, and no dream you can't realize in the form of success with your name attached to it.

All things are possible if you are willing to take action and alter what is critically in need of changing, starting, and ending. These changes help create priceless, gold-star-worthy days that become the shining threads in your coat of honor, clothing you with kindness and compassion toward yourself.

Together we will create an environment utilizing our amazing personal power.

Together we will rise and stand unified for our mutual cause of self-love and respect.

Together we are a part of Team Worthy, striving to win life-embracing self-confidence, pride, and unwavering self-worth.

Let's begin, my worthy warriors, an amazing excursion that will help lift yourself up, reshape your actions, and anchor you to your worth as you prepare to enter a new season in your life, overflowing with splendor.

Self-Realization Toward Change

The purpose of sharing my experience is to reassure you that you are not alone. Many of us have become lost and disconnected from our God-given worthiness. Feeling unworthy disempowers us, saddens our hearts, and clouds our spirits. This in turn leans us toward living a life that does not honor us.

We deserve better. We so deserve much, much better. The only one who can give that precious gift of worth to you is yourself.

We carry our worthiness within us. Our hearts hold the key to releasing their brilliant light, love, and energy. Self-love is an open door, allowing us to cross the threshold into a world of value and respect.

The genesis of your transformation will begin with the evaluation of your beliefs and your decision to change those that don't respect your happiness as sacred. This journey will help you find your way to that beautiful, comfortable place where you can flourish, because what you think, feel, choose, and love matters. It is your safe haven, the place you call home.

I hope the thoughts in this book are inspiring to you as you access your own power for living the life you love and deserve. All your energies are released when your "worthy muscle" gets strengthened. This exercise encourages you to pursue your life's goals that bless and serve your highest good in all matters great and small.

What Do You Feel Worthy of Right Now?

Worthiness is a treasure. Now is the time to open the door to begin your own treasure hunt filled with priceless riches called happiness, serenity, harmony, authenticity, and abundance.

As your mighty and magical gateway, worthiness will lead you to limitless possibilities. This worthy imprint will mark the beautiful new life you're creating for yourself as you continue your virtuous quest in search of your worthy-filled heart overflowing with hope, power, and pride.

This book is a call to attention on feeling and acting upon your intrinsic worth. *It's Never Too Late to Be Worthy Of ...* will lead you to a life of greater importance and encourage your dreams to take root and bloom.

Understanding the importance of self-worth or deservedness is a fundamental but often overlooked element on the road to recovery. You will wake up worthy each morning, trusting in miracles, inspired effort, and sacred opportunities to help make your greatest aspirations come true. This intrinsic awareness is crucial for your ultimate happiness and personal fulfillment.

I realized that even though I had been worthy in certain areas of my life, I needed to develop a deeper recognition of choices I've made that led to unworthy results. It was necessary to view these opposing dynamics in order to move forward in the direction of authentic joy. Uncovering the times I struggled with my worthiness set me on an intimate journey of reflecting, objecting and finally redirecting my path toward a respectable outcome.

In order for my worthy wings to help me take flight, I first had to get out of my own way and still the distractions so I could hear the voices of worthiness ringing in my ears. Until then, I was unable to release my precious energy, allowing it to cultivate my own light, self-love and respect.

I began to remind myself that I had always possessed the power and that I needed to learn to use it again. I had to change the conversations I was having with myself about myself, requiring my attention to be in alignment with my hopes and dreams. Up to that point, I had been depleting my emotional energy on everyone else.

Through these windows of enlightenment, I was able to transform the way I treated others and myself. Bottom line, I had to learn to be worthy. I had to understand that I was obligated to feed my worth with attention, effort, and self-love, which are pivotal for growth and well-being.

Allow me to share with you my personal journey toward living a more worthy life and the steps I took to transcend the life I had settled into over so many years.

*Always with grace and respect for yourself and others

The Rebirth of My Worth: How My Journey Began

My time had come.

It was a Friday in May 2010, and when I awoke that morning, I knew I was never going to be the same. The details of the event aren't important; we all have our own chosen life, a script playing out to a new ending, and this was mine.

It was a complicated weekend filled with a confusing mixture of joy and sorrow. However, a new and unfamiliar sensation emerged, called value—my *own* value . I could feel the anatomy of my heart and mind start to change structure, bringing me from background to foreground and from complacency to taking action.

Although sadness and fear were the initial feelings that greeted me, courage, hope, and providence soon became the navigational energies leading my spirit forward. This epiphany promoted me, allowing me to use the power that I had abandoned long ago.

Emotionally, I had lost my way and had been stuck for too long in my unwillingness to make my needs a priority. Although this event happened in only a moment, that beautiful, priority-filled moment led me to a dazzling acceptance, allowing me to view the many freedoms I had long surrendered. This truth led me out of a stagnant status quo and started my life transformation, which was led by the strength of my now-fearless heart moving me from meek to mighty.

The last straw had been thrown on the pile. The initial ones were of heartache, disappointment, and anger. The final straw unleashing me into action was my own worthiness. I needed to stop fighting *with* myself and start fighting *for* myself.

For the first time in years, my focus wasn't on anyone else. My attention was on me, my honor, and my deservedness of a precious gift called happiness. I wanted more!

I said, "Enough is enough," and finally meant it. I then valiantly began the process of building a brave, new, worthy world embracing the precious gifts of a hope-filled and intentional life. My mission was to recreate my choices in the very next moment, growing into the next hours and days, and to continue to work toward a lifetime reflecting my joyful intentions. I was determined to find my voice, allowing me to speak up on behalf of myself. I needed to challenge my fears and use my own power to build the better life I yearned for but had suppressed for so long.

This became my crusade: to champion a world with happiness, serenity, and fulfillment at the helm of my lifeboat. And thus *It's Never Too Late to Be Worthy Of* ... was born! It is with a full heart and grateful spirit that I release my story to you.

My prayer is that it will help you take flight and will assist you in using your power to earn an authentic and sparkling life overflowing with worthiness.

Your time has come. I invite you to join me in this noble quest.

The Dynamic Forces Influencing Worthiness

Metaphorically, worthiness is a strong, proud, glorious, and leaf-filled willow tree. If we don't cultivate the soil with water, sunshine, and nutrients, it weakens the infrastructure, which soon becomes brittle and barren. We must nurture our soils with love and focus, which will create a bountiful, worthy landscape.

Like the ebb and flow of the ocean, our worthy waters are in constant motion. Similarly, life's interactions create movement and carry weight that directly influences our worth both positively and negatively. These engagements affect the swing of our pendulum toward or away from our center of worthiness. The characteristics unique to each of us also impact our degrees of worth.

Our confidence can be acutely affected by society's judgments. I came to realize that my worthiness is not measured by the possessions I acquire in my life or by the opinions of others, but by something that I needed to access within me. I needed to eliminate the debilitating comparisons I was guilty of making about myself and to distance myself from the ones I allowed others to impose on me. These realizations helped reveal the work that stretched before me.

There are many aspects of deservedness, from the seemingly superficial (not being rushed at the public bathroom hand dryer) to the profound (beginning a brand-new life with our joyful intentions before us). I have witnessed that little, sometimes silly, commonsense entitlements can gently awaken us to our greater wisdom. Left unattended, those nudges become powerful shoves toward the truths we need to accept.

The moral of the story is that we should pay better attention to gentle signs to avoid the more difficult pushes we inevitably encounter if we continue to ignore them. Once your worthy voice speaks up on behalf of you in an audible pitch, changes begin to occur triumphantly. How you arrive at these worthiness crossroads is personal, but once you become aware of them, you can never *not* be aware of them again—not comfortably, at least. This muscle enables us to tackle huge, life-changing events, directing our attention to a newfound self-respect.

Ultimately, the most sacred truth is that we are all God's children and are born worthy. However, many of us become lost in life's twists and turns. My hope is to help you reclaim your God-given worthy heart, allowing the full blooming of your value to become visible to the world. These revelations can guide you to the healing of your injuries and return you to your majestic inception.

This increases confidence and power as you make daily choices while it illuminates your way. Making this worthy imprint reassures you and encourages you to continue moving forward. Many freedoms return to you when you honor and support the integrity of positive and healthy goals.

It is my objective to help you create your own worthy books, leading you into a grace-filled existence with consideration for others without losing sight of yourself.

We should never lose our sense of wonder, because the world is beautiful and exquisite, full of rich possibilities for making our dreams come true. We spend too much time with fragments of worthiness that cause our personal choices to be less than ideal. It's now time for healing ourselves into a more worthy whole.

Any step forward can improve your life and encourage empowerment. This invites greater changes that build and strengthen your foundation. It's a process that takes reflection, time, and energy. Worthiness can be developed with patience and persistence as part of the formula.

Be aware that this process rearranges the dynamics in others' lives as well, from the impatient person behind you at the dryer in the public bathroom to the person who never believed you had the courage, strength, or ability to reinvent a dazzling new life. This effect may create ripples that will surprise those who have known the less-than-worthy you. Remember that these changes are your right as you attempt to rebuild positive standards and worthy practices in your own life.

Choosing to invest in yourself is a sound and critical decision. Always remember that you are not on this journey alone. We are all tenderly connected. I and countless others are by your side. Be comforted in knowing that with the grace of God, anything is possible.

We begin each day by showing up for our worthy work. A newfound embodiment of self-worth makes our new, exquisite, gentler world go around.

Operation Worthy

One of the main objectives of your mission will be to encourage the pressing of your own *reset to worthy button* as you maneuver through decisions in all matters both great and small. To help you along in your worthy campaign, I've created a list of awakenings for you to reflect on and, if relevant, to put into practice to affirm your God-given worthiness. These insights are meant to guide you to consider your current sense of self-worth and how you may feel worthy or unworthy in different situations.

I've also developed applications to lead you through various practical exercises. When applied, this worthy work will strengthen your worthy muscle and increase your insights into new and evolved passageways. Let's begin to look at the worthy side of life and discover all the blessings and grace that are there for your choosing.

Take what applies, ignore what doesn't, and then break it down into easy steps.

Decide what stays and what goes, who you keep close and who you keep at a distance, where you spend your time and where you don't, and when you give, when you keep, when you take. Ultimately this will tip the balance of importance to your side as you create your very own circle of support.

Let us now build a positive and compassionate alliance as we grow strong together.

Worthy Awakenings

It's never too late to be worthy ...

Of reading this book to explore the wonderful things you deserve to be worthy of.

Of placing yourself at the top (or at least in the top three) of your list of priorities.

Of happiness with your name attached to it.

Of blue skies and cool kisses.

Of sweet dreams and ice cream.

Of happy heart and healthy soul.

Of playing music you want to listen to.

Of good food energizing your mind as well as your body.

Of a money flow that pays the bills with a bit extra.

Of calm seas and easy chairs to plop into.

Of warm hugs by a glowing fireplace.

Of staying in bed as long as you'd like to once in a while.

Of those eyes to gaze into that you can truly trust.

Of a family who appreciates you.

Of "the talk" needing to be had.

Of considering your needs before all others in the personal decisions you have to make.

Of saying *no* and meaning it.

Of saying *yes* and meaning it.

Of saying "we will see" and not being pressured to say no *or* yes.

Of hugging, hugging, and hugging some more and not being the first one to end the hug.

Of spreading the peanut butter slowly and evenly to the edges of *your* sandwich.

Of waiting until a favorite song finishes before exiting the car.

Of joy squared.

Of joy to the power of three.

Of finding the love of your life in this moment in your life.

Of crying because it makes you feel better.

Of asking for necessary favors.

Of teaching or reteaching yourself what you need to be taught in spite of your fears and resistance.

Of walking confidently and proudly down the worthy side of the street.

Of reacting to challenging encounters with worthy words and a tone that earns attention and respect.

Of saying no to ridiculous favors asked of you.

Of not having to explain yourself when privacy is a necessary element.

Of praying, meditating, and being present in your own life.

Of just being.

Of witnessing the sun's glorious movement, both rising and setting, with hope-filled expectancy of blessed and worthy things.

Of watching in full attention the grass grow, the snow fall, the waves crash, and the fire dance.

Of going makeup free or "putting on the dog."

Of expecting the best outcome in a situation and not settling for less.

Of not caring to compete or justify, because the universe has an abundant life for us all.

Of being tired and not pushing through it but rather resting.

Of feeling what you're feeling so you can release it into the gentle arms of the universe.

Of reapplying coats of courage because it makes you feel stronger.

Of changing what needs to be changed while protecting what needs to remain the same.

It's never too late to be worthy ...

Of wearing smaller jeans with your shirt fearlessly tucked in.

Of slaying the dragons blocking your dreams.

Of having the courage to triple-dog dare yourself.

Of being free of guilt over things you should not feel guilty about.

Of just breathing.

Of following your dreams.

Of removing the toxic energy in your life.

Of winning the lottery because someone has to win it, and you actually did buy a ticket.

Of receiving the same tolerance you extend tenderly to others.

Of going to sleep and staying asleep.

Of being grateful for the blessings surrounding you.

Of placing your invisible crown on your head as you live this day royally.

Of objecting when you have a right to.

Of finally allowing others to be their *own* heroes in their life stories.

Of embracing the dreams you're willing to put work boots on to achieve.

Of the recognition and respect you deserve for sharing your talent to create a better world.

Of not caring what the neighbors will say (or do say).

Of being your own best friend.

Of making sure if you're going to be a people- pleaser that you are one of the people you please.

Of not apologizing when you did nothing wrong.

Of learning the lessons life keeps trying to teach you.

Of not keeping up with the Jones's (unless you want to) or deciding to surpass them and not just keep up with them.

Of brushing your teeth with intention and repetition, really slowly.

Of turning off the cell phone so you can have precious uninterrupted moments of silence.

Of knowing all your friendships are not created equal.

Of realizing that the people in your life need to earn their relationship with you.

Of investing time, energy, and money in your own needs.

Of someone saving a seat for you once in a while.

Of not being the first one to volunteer all the time.

Of having the right to be heard without needing to win.

Of reminding people when they owe you money.

Of not giving away the praise.

Of graciously taking and accepting the credit.

Of speaking slowly and thoughtfully, even when someone is rushing you.

Of "playing it forward" into your life script and realizing the truth of a situation.

Of not being "on duty" on your day off.

Of reteaching people how to treat you by changing the conversation.

Of putting your eggs in as many baskets, buckets, and containers as you choose.

Of taking the road most traveled every now and then.

Of finally giving yourself the advantage in a situation.

Of being totally committed to your mission by bravely loving yourself enough to change.

Of moving forward armed with all the instruments necessary to reach a productive, powerful, and positive outcome.

Of telling someone exactly what to bring as a guest when asked, instead of saying, "Nothing." (You know who you are.)

Of using two expensive tea bags in one cup of tea.

It's never too late to be worthy ...

Of not always needing to be the hero for everyone else and allowing others to learn this precious power for themselves.

Of admitting, "I'm not sure what I think."

Of talking to who you need to talk to with entitlement, clarity, and conviction.

Of not giving permission to someone else to qualify your worth, but to feel entitled to recognize your own value in light of your amazing talents.

Of speaking up with your worthy voices the things that need to be heard, respected, and understood.

Of not being the only one divulging the financial details in the relationship.

Of being told "thank you" for going out of your way.

Of eating your food at the table with a knife and fork instead of standing and grazing at the refrigerator door.

Of splitting the cost right down the middle instead of rounding the number to your disadvantage.

Of ordering dessert when no one else is ordering it.

Of not ordering dessert when everyone else is ordering it.

Of hiding the last ripe banana for yourself.

Of not drinking from the flat, bubbleless, improperly closed bottle of soda.

Of keeping the important family memento and not passing it to someone else.

Of standing up for yourself when someone attempts to push you down.

Of telling someone, "Yes, you did wake me up."

Of taking that calculated risk because the positive outcome is greater than the negative status quo you're trapped in.

Of knowing your worth and not settling for less.

Of asking someone else to run the errand.

Of accepting the money back that is owed to you instead of saying, "Don't worry about it."

Of not saying, "It's fine," when it isn't.

Of not being the first person to say hello all the time.

Of not choosing to explain or defend your decisions.

Of setting your own pace so you will always be the winner of your life race.

Of your own personal resurrection from a life not authentically lived.

Of picking up the pieces of your life and remaking it into a whole new masterpiece.

Of spending quality time *with* yourself, not by yourself.

Of investing in your future instead of supporting everyone else's present.

Of cooking chicken soup with long-grain rice for your benefit too.

Of taking time in the morning to wake up, sip coffee slowly, and dress with intention.

Of normal blood pressure.

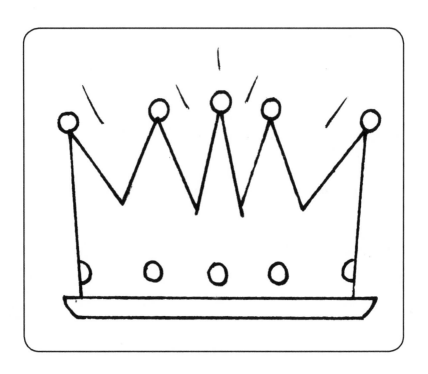

Of wearing the crown in your
life that comes from living
authentically with worth, courage,
and grace.

Of someone else picking up the lunch tab now and then.

Of a hot cup of tea being made just for you.

Of an all-expense-paid trip to Hawaii, Italy, wherever.

Of diamond-studded anything.

Of receiving the "how are *you* feeling" call instead of always being the caring caller.

Of a blessed rite of passage into a more worthy "whole."

Of being thanked for a job well done.

Of worry-free financial serenity.

Of chilling in a car with the sun streaming through the window on a cold winter day, contemplating what you are worthy of.

Of counting and recounting your blessings.

Of making your own life magic, which fills your soul with satisfaction.

Of finally receiving the apology with your name attached to it, thereby allowing your heart to move to a gentler place.

Of knowing that on the other side of our endings we can build brilliant new beginnings.

It's never too late to be worthy ...

Of embracing your spiritual royalty that allows you to live a life blessed with honor and internal wealth.

Of dancing fearlessly and confidently while everyone's watching.

Of singing off-key and loudly—and not only in the shower.

Of naming those precious angels surrounding and supporting your life's daily rounds.

Of bringing to life your mom's dreams left unrealized during her life.

Of discovering the treasure awaiting you by trusting in the path of your life map.

Of trusting in God's miracles, your inspired effort, and the universe's sacred opportunities to help make your dreams come true.

Of forgiveness for your shortcomings as you in turn forgive others for theirs.

Of being the champion of your own heart and loving yourself unconditionally.

Of not just getting a score of 100 percent on the "life test" but finally passing the course.

Of understanding that being stressed and healthy, instead of stressed and unhealthy, is still an improvement.

Of defending your life.

Of crossing those life bridges you so critically need to cross and bringing yourself to a better place on the other side.

Of answering back with strength, grace, respect, and entitlement.

Of surviving the storm by passing through it to the other side and into sunlight.

Of getting down on your knees and thanking God for all the pain and trauma you've escaped.

Of slowing down.

Of stepping back.

Of leaping forward.

Of pressing your reset button to bring you back to that good place you wandered away from.

Of finding your own true north by abandoning the familiar but dangerous untrue south.

Of taking the time to exercise consistently.

Of making peace with your comfortable, happy, and healthy body because you are living an authentic life that honors you on the inside so you can reflect it on the outside.

Of getting to pick the next movie you both see.

Of doing nothing—I repeat *nothing*—on your days off.

Of disappointing someone else on behalf of not disappointing yourself for a change.

Of acknowledging the flow of God's daily grace into the stream of your life.

Of writing your own book, which makes it to number one on the *New York Times* bestseller list.

Of those blessed minutes with your name securely attached to them.

Of experiencing spectacular blue-skied, sunshiny days within yourself, even when it's rainy, cold, and cloudy outside, because you are living worthy.

Of remembering *your* food items on the shopping list.

Of making a special trip back to the store for the items you forgot to get for yourself.

Of achieving the tender balance in your life between work and play as well as between what you keep and give away.

Of expecting the people in your life to be interested in the unfolding of your dreams and goals.

Of talking with someone to get the help you need, even if it means paying for it.

Of embracing the healing instead of continuing the bruising.

Of going public with your healing process instead of staying private with your wounds.

Of saying, "Enough is enough," and finally meaning it.

Of telling yourself, "I am asking too much of myself."

Of asking for special accommodations under special circumstances.

Of switching your service provider because their performance is not pleasing to you.

Of shooting for the moon and actually getting the lifelong win.

Of finally understanding that one size *never did* fit all and never will.

Of asking, asking, asking until you get an answer.

Of honoring how tired you feel instead of dismissing it.

Of being entitled to tell people
they are asking too much of you.

Of taking your time at the public bathroom dryer until your hands are completely dry instead of feeling the pressure from others behind you.

Of finally agreeing graciously with the recognition you are receiving.

Of creating a sacred space to pray, meditate, and give thanks for the joys in your life.

Of filling your joy bucket each and every day.

Of wearing your most expensive cologne to go errand schlepping.

It's never too late to be worthy ...

Of not saving your new necklace for a special occasion.

Of telling someone that what he or she is proposing is *totally unacceptable.*

Of fighting *for* yourself instead of *with* yourself.

Of asking for what you need with clear and specific detail.

Of surprising others regarding your new and unfamiliar decisions, which serve you and stand in direct contrast to their assumptions.

Of rising above your doubts, fears, and insecurities to achieve your wildest dreams.

Of following your bliss.

Of waking up worthy.

Of creating your very own wish list to communicate exactly the gift you wish to receive (even if you aren't asked).

Of getting ahead of yourself—in fact, far, far ahead of yourself—in dreams, work, passion, play, and love.

Of taking your time at the eye exam to decide which screen is clearer, even if it means going over and over the choices.

Of returning to the front of the line at the post office after you were sent to the back counter for additional paperwork, despite the annoyed looks of the people behind you.

Of taking your time to verify and put your cash away when checking out at the supermarket.

Of sending back to the kitchen the improperly prepared salad or entrée, even if it means dining alone at the table when everyone else is finished.

Of finally buying yourself the "red Corvette" you've always longed for.

Of checking out any time you'd like and then actually leaving.

Of deciding against the popular vote.

Of refusing the job offer and not feeling pressured into accepting it.

Of creating your own vision board with your joys, hopes, and dreams mapped out on it.

Of believing in miracles, magic, and grace.

Of not going with the flow but against the current, because that is where your dreams lie buried.

Of choosing at the crossroads the direction best serving your needs.

Of allowing your fear to guide you to the appropriate response and defense.

Of taking a mental health day from life once in a while so you can go out and play.

Of saying and sticking by your "no thank you."

Of the freedom experienced while protecting worthiness in all matters great or small.

Of allowing the voicemail to screen your calls.

Of making a pot of soup to comfort yourself through a blizzard.

Of listening to your favorite music or watching your favorite TV show.

Of the right of refusal without any explanation.

Of saying what you are talented at—out loud and to other people.

Of winning your own victories.

Of finally realizing you are born and blessed with royal, worthy blood flowing through your veins.

Of telling someone, "Hold on," "Wait a minute, I have someone on the other line," "Can't talk now," "It's not a good time."

Of doing things in the order of their importance.

Of asking someone else to _____ instead of you always being the doer.

Of knowing not all things are created equal in importance.

Of clearly and consistently being able to identify your greater good in a situation.

Of editing your usual guest list to reduce complications.

It's never too late to be worthy ...

Of delaying the visit because it doesn't easily work into your day.

Of initiating the uncomfortable reminder face-to-face.

Of deciding not to answer the question quickly or even get back to the phone message until you can process a thoughtful response.

Of speaking your piece as well as listening to theirs.

Of not saying "I'm sorry" when the other person bumped into you.

Of going first safely during a car stand-off on a narrow road.

Of not giving up the private details to an inquisitive questioner.

Of doing a quick cleanup when short on time—and not feeling guilty about it.

Of taking your time on an entrance ramp of a parkway until you feel it is the right moment to proceed, despite impatient drivers behind you.

Of requesting a complementary car wash when having your car serviced.

Of telling a white lie to protect someone's feelings from being hurt.

Of being protective of the tender balance between movement and stillness.

Of telling the gift giver—gently, of course—that the garment wasn't the right size.

Of knowing you already have within you the courage, wisdom, and power to live the life you love.

Of giving yourself permission to be sick, feel sick, and therefore act sick.

Of surrendering all tasks, lists, and errands when not feeling well.

Of "obeying" being ill and solely resting, relinquishing responsibilities to everyone else.

Of not revealing your fashion secrets or the name of your hairdresser.

Of complaining when accommodations are not up to par.

Of asking for more *anything*.

Of checking on your persistent cough by giving in and seeing the doctor.

Of lounging until noon in your pj's on a sweet, cold Sunday.

Of insisting to speak directly to the doctor when on the follow-up call.

Of not letting the error go without respectfully discussing it.

Of not turning the financial cheek.

Of protecting your precious free time rather than the money offered to work during it.

Of dry-cleaning your favorite jeans.

Of respecting silence in a conversation instead of jumping in to break it.

Of doing unto yourself as you do unto others.

Of not turning the other cheek over and over again but standing firmly in your position or even turning and walking away.

Of playfully looking in the mirror and saying, "Who's better than me?"

Of defending the unfairly accused one.

Of accusing the guilty defended one.

Of yielding instead of stopping or going.

Of asking the workers to wipe their feet before entering your clean house.

Of eating with grace and honor to bless bodies, souls, and spirits.

Of taking a power nap in the middle of the day to recharge your body's batteries.

Of saying good morning with eye contact and a smile when you enter an elevator of strangers waiting to catch your blessing when they respond back.

Of blooming where you are
planted, wherever you are
right now.

Of stopping and not only smelling the roses, but also creating a beautiful bouquet to enjoy and cherish.

Of not taking the lesser of the two evils, but the greater of the two blessings.

Of objecting to rude and ungrateful behavior.

Of doing the work necessary to get to the desired result.

Of changing your mind midstream.

Of being present in the conversation even when there are one million things you "need" to do.

Of driving slowly in the slow lane.

Of driving the speed limit in the middle lane.

Of wearing pants with a snap and zipper instead of an elastic waistband or wearing pants with an elastic waistband instead of a snap and zipper.

Of simply saying "thank you" when someone compliments you.

Of saying you love it when everyone else hates it.

It's never too late to be worthy ...

Of saying you hate it when everyone else loves it.

Of not taking the blame when it isn't your fault.

Of raising or lowering the thermostat for your own comfort level.

Of not initiating the let's-get-together statement unless you truly *want* to get together.

Of searching, switching, and searching some more until you find the treatment you deserve.

Of treating yourself to the most expensive toothbrush on the shelf.

Of the same entitlement given to everyone else.

Of not holding your life's joys and serenity hostage by having unrealistic deadlines, expectations and standards.

Of loyalty to yourself in all things.

Of refueling with reverence and gratitude.

Of reestablishing your emotional equilibrium by honoring what you're feeling.

Of being the champion in your world's arena.

Of living an authentic life surrounded by authentic truths.

Of looking in the mirror with pride at the person smiling back.

Of inner peace because of the outer work you are willing to do.

Of being aware of your everyday epiphanies.

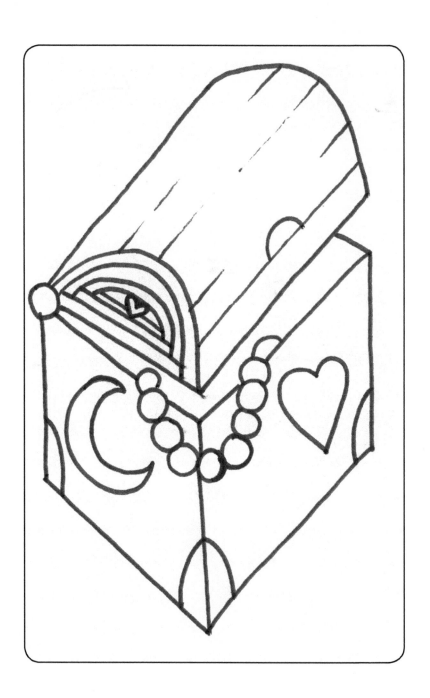

Of never losing your sense of wonder because the world is too beautiful and exquisite, with rich possibilities for making your dreams come true.

Of joyfulness in all your days—easy as well as difficult ones.

Of making up your own mind based on research, comfort level, and common sense.

Of organizing the comfortable rhythm of your life's daily routines.

Of believing "in faith" that all things are possible.

Of expecting stunning success.

Of being a visionary of great things in your life.

Of being enthusiastic about the life you're currently living as well as the new one stretching before you.

Of embracing all the good things you hope for.

Of dodging the curve balls aimed squarely at your head.

Of justice in all matters.

Of knowing you will not be "convicted by a jury of your peers," because they have walked in your shoes.

Of harmony and its holy energies blessing you.

Of opening "new doors" (when you hear the knocking), with anticipation, courage, and hope for exciting new opportunities.

Of those precious, holy unscripted moments of bliss.

Of loving yourself with abandon and without conditions.

Of surrendering the rigid illusion of control and replacing it with the more fluid and flexible truth called "manage."

Of surviving and surpassing life's tests with dignity, integrity, and prayer.

Of weaving your life tapestry with brilliant colors.

Of hearing "I am here for you for whatever you need" instead of always being the one saying it.

Of being afraid of the big bad wolf because self-protection is a gift that can keep you safe.

It's never too late to be worthy ...

Of believing that anything is possible—and I do mean *anything.*

Of not finishing everything on your plate or finishing everything on your plate without needing to comment about it.

Of putting only your name on the gift card instead of including all the noncontributing others.

Of not fixing everyone else's problems but allowing them the ownership, maturity, and growth to do their own life work.

Of using your own comfortable timing to make the left turn, disregarding anyone else's coaxing or honking to do so before you are ready to do it safely.

NO REGRETS

Of having no regrets for decisions made and actions performed on your own behalf.

Of this being the year that all your dreams take root, bloom, and begin to blossom.

Of inventing a million-dollar product to retire on.

Of making a short story long just because you feel like it.

Of wearing "leopard"—and all that loudly and beautifully implies.

Of being open to new experiences that enlarge your life's résumé.

Of not responding to the rude text and letting "loud silence" speak volumes.

Of eating that cannoli without defense or apology.

Of leaving a note for people to clean up after themselves.

Of requesting to be served by your favorite teller in the bank.

Of finally agreeing with the praise people give you regarding your wisdom, your talent, and your gifts.

Of not waiting for perfect conditions to chase your dreams—or you won't get anything done.

Of reflection, objection, and then redirection.

Of the life you are creating being worthy of you.

Of taking the precious time to do an inspired yoga practice that is prayer with your body and enlightening to your soul.

Of celebrating your true friends, who encourage you to live your days with courage, optimism, and joy.

Of conquering your self-limiting beliefs.

Of answering God's calling for you to use your talents on behalf of others, providing hope for their dreams to come true.

Of resting peacefully and safely in the knowledge that God has you in the palm of His hand (Isaiah 49).

Of being worthy of yourself.

Of trusting in Jesus' message "Therefore I tell you, whatever you ask for in prayer, believe that you have received it and it will be yours" (Mark 11:24).

Of being worthy. Amen.

How Did Your Worthiness Weigh In?

The wonderful news is that just one changed thought, decision, or action will begin to tip the worthy scale in your favor. You can start only where you are and with what you have, knowing that your newfound realizations will lead you forward to your more worthy presence in the world.

Your Personal Commitment

In your heart, feel the reasons you are deserving of embracing healing and reconnection with your worthiness. Go to your emotional strengths to guide you to the work you need to do to live the beautiful life you deserve.

Make a promise to yourself:

It's Never Too Late For Me To Be Worthy Of...

SIGNATURE　　　　DATE

Healing Ceremonies

Congratulations, my worthy warriors! You now have completed the reading of my awakenings designed to help you recognize the varying levels of worthiness impacted by the different emotions and situations in your life.

In the healing ceremonies that follow, I've distilled many of the lessons I share from my years of personal journeying. It is my hope that you, too, will benefit from moving your worthiness from the background to the foreground.

I welcome you to take the next step forward!

Healing Ceremonies of Worthiness are restorative practices. They can raise your consciousness by guiding you through activities that mend and bless your spirits.

By practicing these rituals in your daily rounds, you can deepen your understanding of "living worthy."

So let's begin together.

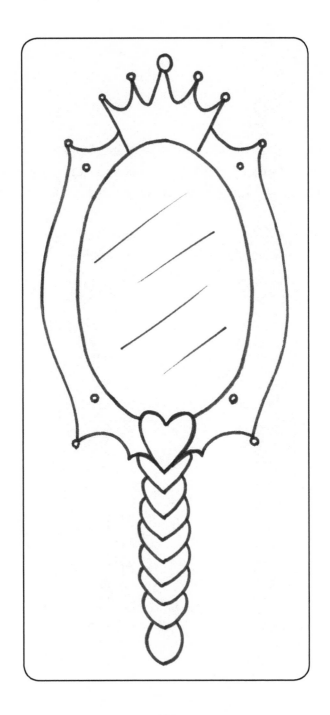

Worthy Mirror Mantra

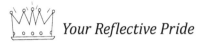 *Your Reflective Pride*

What you say to yourself feeds the power behind the messages you receive. A tender and loving voice delivers the words you deserve and need to hear.

This ceremony is called the *Worthy Mirror Mantra*.

- 💜 Any time throughout your day that you catch your reflection, repeat (to yourself or aloud as appropriate) with enthusiasm: "Mirror, mirror on the wall, I am looking good and standing tall, for I am *worthy* after all."

Begin to feel more vital and important with each worthy statement you make.

Worthy Notes: Extra Credit

When you initially look in the mirror each day, place your invisible crown on your head while reciting the Worthy Mirror Mantra.

As you view your reflection throughout the day, adjust your crown as needed, ensuring it remains securely in its rightful place.

Create your own unique mantra that specifically reflects your own goals and desires.

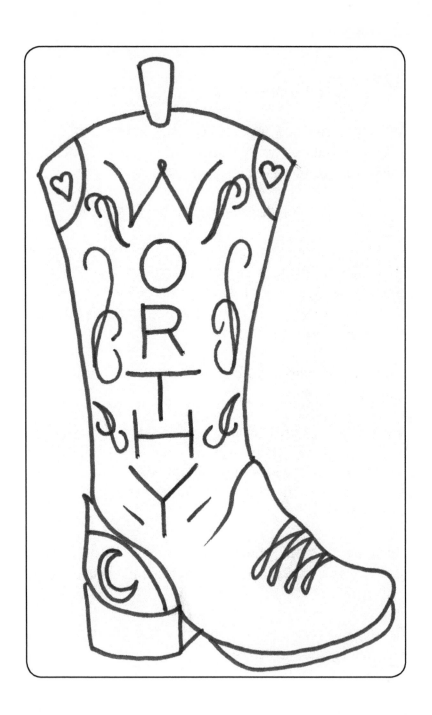

130

Worthy Boots

 *Your Worthy Footsteps*

The steps you take each day mark your path with a specific distinction. Let's make your pace generous, entitled, and loving.

This ceremony is called *Worthy Boots.*

- ♥ Assign a pair of boots or shoes to be used as a symbolic reminder of positive energy and movement.
- ♥ Label each boot or shoe, calling one "worthy" and one "boots."
- ♥ Place them by your front door to remind yourself to put them on as you begin your day with pride and grace.

Begin to feel your energized stride ignite every positive step you take throughout your travels.

Book of Worthy

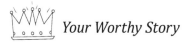 *Your Worthy Story*

Everyone has both pride and glory, so let this be the start of your own story.

This ceremony is called *Book of Worthy*.

- 💜 Choose the form of book you'll use (such as spiral, composition, or loose leaf).
- 💜 Select a photo of yourself reflecting joy and serenity, to be used on the cover.
- 💜 Place powerful and positive words (such as *bloom*, *love*, *believe*, *worthy*) around your photo.
- 💜 Select an awakening that you would like to work on.
- 💜 Journal your intentions by completing this sentence: Right now, I will embrace my worthiness by _____.

Examples:

- Praying, meditating, and being present in your own life
- Not caring to compete or justify, because the universe has an abundant life for us all
- Changing what needs to be changed while protecting what needs to remain the same
- Creating your own vision board with your joys, hopes, and dreams mapped out on it

Begin to feel empowered by the life scripts you are rewriting to support your noble quest of living worthy.

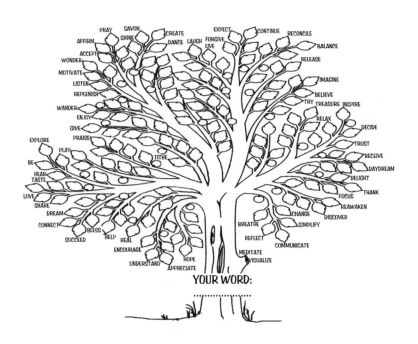

YOUR WORD:
....

Worthy Driven Days

 *Your Worthy Design*

Having spent many years in reflection on my less-than-worthy days, I was able to create the awakenings I share with you. Now it's time to take *your* individual path and create the revelations necessary for recovery.

Days will turn into weeks and then months of "worthy driven" efforts. As you engage differently with yourself and others, in work and at play, at home as well as within your communities, you'll begin to experience beautiful and healing holy moments.

As you may realize by now, to achieve anything in life you have to feel worthy of both making the effort required and receiving the prize desired. This practice becomes the magic I refer to throughout this book.

Time is a finite element. No matter how much we may desire that a given day be longer or pass more quickly, there will always be the same twenty-four hours to spend each and every day. Many of us get caught in the uncomfortable crossfire between chasing time and being chased by it. Coincidentally, these are two versions of the same problem.

However, we do have the power to allocate how we spend our precious energy, allowing us to make the rhythm of each day more comfortable.

This fragile balance can be kept by doing these three important things:

1. delegating tasks to others so you can attend to your needs
2. reprioritizing the items on your to-do list, ensuring you are moving closer to the top of it
3. adapting your standards to fit shifting circumstances

I invite you to begin *your* journey by designing your own worthy-driven days. It is my wish that you be as blessed as I have been in being open to this transformation.

This ceremony is called *Worthy-Driven Days.*

- ♥ Refer to the *take time to* willow tree for ideas of actions you may initiate for unleashing your magic. This can be done daily, weekly, or whenever you choose.
- ♥ Circle a positive action you wish to *take time to* introduce into your day.
- ♥ Write the word in your Book of Worthy.
- ♥ Recognize and initiate opportunities in which you can extend to yourself or others the powerful energy surrounding the action.
- ♥ At the end of the day, review how you *took time to* live a more worthy driven day, and include that in your *Book of Worthy.*

Examples:

- Today I took time to laugh, dance, and treasure the feelings of joy.
- Today I took time to daydream about life's wonder and possibilities.
- Today I took time to pray and thank God for my beautiful life.
- Today I took time to help my community by volunteering.

Begin to feel the fulfillment that accompanies the courage to reflect on and direct new actions encompassing people, places, and things in your worthy triumph.

Scattering Worth

Giving the Gift of Worth

In your day-to-day exchanges with others, expressing their value to them enlarges their esteem and blesses you both.

This ceremony is called *Scattering Worth*.

- ♥ Initiate a communication with a person you know or someone whose life path you crossed who has touched you in some way that made a smile come to your heart.
- ♥ Share your gratitude or praise with them using descriptive words and an enthusiastic tone.
- ♥ Be present in the magical exchange of gratitude and joy between you and the person.
- ♥ Journal your encounters in your Book of Worthy.

Example:

- Today I scattered worth to my florist, Rose, by thanking her for the beautiful bouquet she made for me. I complimented the bright and vibrant colors she chose and the recommendation of flowers she offered. I thanked her for sharing her artistic talent with me.

Begin to feel your joy soar with this beautiful exchange. Remembering the encounter throughout your day will bring a smile to your face and glee to your heart.

Worthy Notes: Extra Credit

Extend praise and thanks to those you may have difficulty relating to in your day-to-day comings and goings.

Don't keep track or use a scorecard as you initiate and generously scatter worth. This will open the universal floodgates, making the planet a kinder, gentler, and more forgiving place.

Welcome and be grateful for the worth
others scatter to you.

Give yourself daily doses of your worth. This practice will be an incredible tool in helping you build confidence.

Worthy Well

 *Your Worthy Vessel*

In pursuit of a more worth-filled heart, your days will overflow with liberties, power, and rewards. Filling yourself with greater entitlements increases self-regard.

This ceremony is called the *Worthy Well*.

- 💜 Select a vessel (such as a bucket, bag, or bowl) and place it in a visible spot.
- 💜 Keep a pad of paper and pen alongside your vessel.
- 💜 Write a "worthy" you have accomplished.
- 💜 Fill your well with these worthy wins.

Begin to feel the increasing power, strength, and self-respect as your well fills with the positive energy accompanying these changes.

Healing Regrets

Reflection and Release

Regret is a useless energy that drains your positive outlook and strength. In life, you are called to endure many tests, and you make decisions that, in their time, seem to make the most sense.

Viewing your past through the eyes of your current circumstance is unfair; you don't see all the details that influenced your choice at that time.

One of your most significant works is learning to have no regrets—or at least fewer of them. To reflect instead of regret is a gift. Seeking newfound and current wisdom for future choices enables you to move onward.

This ceremony is called *Healing Regrets*.

- ❤ Close your eyes, place your hand over your heart, and remind yourself that you did the best you could at that moment.
- ❤ Say a prayer asking for grace and gentleness on behalf of your heart's memory concerning the situation you are struggling with.

Begin to feel your soul soften and your wounds heal, helping you to reconcile past decisions.

Summary of the Seven Healing Ceremonies

Now that you've completed the Seven Healing Ceremonies, it's my hope that these practices have opened the door to a life filled with the increased value of, appreciation for, and validation of how amazing you are!

Let's reflect on your learning.

As you recite your *Worthy Mirror Mantra*, may you see the beautiful person you truly are.

As you put on your *Worthy Boots* when you begin each day, may your footsteps take you to higher, gentler ground.

As you create your own *Book of Worthy*, may your story be filled with love and grace.

As you take time to develop your *Worthy-Driven Days*, may you root yourself in positive forward movement.

As you *Scatter Worth* to others as well as to yourself, may the value you communicate bless those hearts in need of their own truths.

As you fill your *Worthy Well* with confidence, honor, and esteem, may your spirit overflow with hope and reward.

As you *Heal Your Regrets*, may your soul fly free of burdens and sadness, embracing understanding, forgiveness, and acceptance.

Build a Worthy Foundation

To further increase your power, I have outlined practical steps for building a worthy foundation. The durability of a structure is determined by its foundation's stability. When we build our platform on spiritual beliefs as well as practical efforts, the result is extremely blessed and powerful. To help you with this, let me introduce you to the *Golden Worthy Rules and Considerations.*

Golden Worthy Rules

- Write a gratitude list daily to connect with the blessings surrounding you every day.
- Get a good night's sleep to recharge your energy and focus.
- Share your abundance and generosity with others to pay forward good will, charity, and service.
- Pray, reflect, and be willing to work toward changes that will move your life forward into worthiness and joy.
- Embrace your Healing Ceremonies of Worthiness, and experience the magic these rituals unleash.

- Keep the people who support you nearby to surround you with gentleness, love, and hope while you compassionately forgive those who are unable to be what you wish them to be.
- Refill your joy buckets and play enthusiastically to replenish your center and add glee to your heart.
- Eat healthy food, and move a little more every day to honor your body as well as your spirit.
- Breathe, be present, and be worthy in all things.
- Extend love to others as well as back to yourself.
- Believe in your dreams as you live authentically and exuberantly in pursuit of them each day.
- Design realistic, positive goals to bless your life with energy and forward movement.
- Draw necessary lines in your sand to uphold peace, harmony, and balance in your own life.

Worthy Considerations

Be open to sources of information and guidance (such as support groups, self-help tools, legal counsel, and financial advice).

Parting Thoughts: Beginning Your Journey

Bravo, my worthy warriors! I am so very proud of the fearless way you have approached this expedition in search of your worthy selves.

It has been my honor and privilege to be your guide. Although we will part ways to follow the paths leading to our unique personal intentions, always remember we are tenderly connected as we continue to work side by side to sustain our successful worthy quest.

The key to consistent dedication and the execution of this work will be driven by the magnitude of your desire to achieve these precious goals. Therefore, my greatest hope is that what I've shared here can help you find your way back home to the place of the undeniable truth that *we are all born worthy.*

During our lives, many times our essence is injured. It is our right to heal through new decisions and actions we make to bless our worthy redesigned lives. With God by our side, using His grace as our guide, anything is possible! This belief becomes our gateway to being entitled to pursuing our most beautiful dreams.

Our precious and fragile worthiness lies in our own very powerful and capable hands. Living worthy is a decision. The choices we make, the ones we choose not to make, the effort we invest, and the irrefutable faith we must have lead the way to a consistent, thriving, and authentic lifestyle.

Gratitude, generosity, love, and forgiveness bring us to our highest good and bless our days.

I personally discovered in these past years that I need to make the decision every day to wake up worthy. I must earn a life of respect and value by understanding the part I play in directing and protecting that life. Now, as I continue to sort and sift through my thoughts and emotions as well as practice my healing ceremonies, my natural inclinations are instinctively worthy.

I pray that when you are called to your altar of worthy, you embrace the spiritual birthright of having been made in the image and likeness of God, accepting your divine legacy of priorities, privilege, and importance in all matters, because it's never too late to continue your own journey of living worthy.

I now understand that I share in the responsibility of living in grace with others as a way of honoring God's unconditional and loving grace for me. I wish you grace. Wish some for me too!

Here is a prayer to send you on your way as you continue your personal odyssey:

My Sweet Worthy

Thank You, dear God, for reminding me that I am Your beloved child and already have the courage, strength, and wisdom needed to believe I am deserving of the new and joyful life I am creating.

Let me always remain grateful for Your love, Your light, and Your protection that bless my life always. Guide my actions to make an ever-greater difference in the world by helping me hear Your divine whispers, ensuring that I live my life with the purpose You intend.

Knowing that *I was born worthy*, it's never too late to *feel* worthy of Your divine gifts, which fill and surround my life each and every day. Amen.

As you follow your path, always believe in God's miracles, your inspired efforts, and the universe's sacred opportunities for helping your dreams to come true. May your precious, worthy hearts love you, lift you, and lead you to kinder and gentler places where your hopes and wishes can take root and bloom; a worthy-celebrated life.

Never forget that you are entitled to leading the incredible life you imagine and so deserve to have.

We are all forever worthy of our "happily ever after."

Living a Worthy Celebrated Life

Beginning with the fateful day that providence, worthiness and acceptance led me on a mission to recreate a life of greater happiness, I am joyous to share with you that I have earned back my "crown", living authentically with faith, courage and worth.

My most valuable revelation has been learning to protect that "crown" every day with the grace filled and critical choices I make, respecting my needs and desires in addition to honoring the considerations I give generously to others.

*Always with grace and respect for yourself and others

Blessings and Gratitude

Although it was my personal journey that created this book's truths and revelations, it was God, my precious family, and my dearest friends who gave my sweet Worthy her wings! It was their love, support, and encouragement that helped me to move forward bravely and confidently with *It's Never Too Late to Be Worthy Of* ...

These writings didn't come from me but rather through me. My transformation began on that fateful day in May when Jesus rescued me, and my worthiness was reborn and given a voice. It is with humility and great appreciation that this divine collaboration was formed.

Among my many life's treasures is my best friend, Val, whose devotion, generosity, humor, and respect of my journey helped bring this book into its polished form. Her amazing cognitive as well as creative talents blessed my work. I am forever a better person because of our friendship and am beyond thankful to know her. Our futures look bright as we anticipate new dreams coming true.

To my sweetheart, James, whose belief in me elevated my confidence to continue with my dream of helping others live a life of increased worthiness. He forever cheers me forward to embrace blessings in all things that are precious to me. Because of his support and love, my Worthy has been released to the world.

Love and thanks to my three incredible daughters, Kristin, Stephanie, and Lauren, who always courageously and independently walk to the beat of their unique drums. I taught them to follow their dreams, believing that they could come true when accompanied by hard work and self-love. My love has no conditions when it comes to them. They have supported my Worthy with their creative genius and their formatting, marketing, and technical skills. Kristin lent her artistic soul to exploring new multifaceted dimensions within these pages. Stephanie lent her enlightened spirit to help manifest this book's message to its highest good. Lauren lent her loving heart to add colorful energy to its beautiful content.

Merci to my son-in-law François, who extended his talents to the conceptual design of our work as well as adding his "French touch" to many of our brainstorming sessions.

Endless thanks to Michael, who generously shared his amazing artistic talent and time to draw the illustrations within these pages.

Immeasurable appreciation to Team Moonblooms for the donation of their time, efforts, and talents. Bless you, Valerie Rusinak, James Cammarata, Kristin S. Vera, Stephanie Rose Speranza, Lauren Doppler-Speranza, François Doppler-Speranza, and Michael Laurence Vera.

In honor of my mom and dad, who always taught me to be strong, positive, and goal-oriented as well as to believe I could triumph over my challenges with prayer, hope, and focus. They also encouraged my enthusiasm and motivated me to take my endeavors to a successful win. Their upbringing provided the foundation upon which I forged my path with strength and bravery. I continue to build on that foundation with authenticity and worthiness by my side.

A loving thank you to my mom in heaven, who always believed that two wrongs would never make a right and that we should treat others as we would have them treat us. Always taking the high road, she was surrounded by a beautiful light that touched upon those who were blessed to know her. She was a woman well ahead of her time who embraced her own holistic and spiritual awakenings in search of her greatest truths. She shared her talent and wisdom unconditionally, making the world a kinder and gentler place. Living the doctrines of tithing and paying it forward, her contributions to those less fortunate were touchstone's to her life's philosophy. Mom, you are such a part of me in this book; we took this journey together, tenderly connected by our hearts and the belief that everyone is entitled to living a worthy-celebrated life.

An enthusiastic thank-you to my dad, who earned a Purple Heart for bravery in World War II. As a young girl, he shared with me the positive teachings of Dr. Norman Vincent Peale, Napoleon Hill, and Earl Nightingale. He continues to share with me his unending mantras: "Do more than what is expected of you" and "Depend upon yourself to make the good things happen in your life." He is one of the greatest motivators of my success as far as my memory extends. He also has always believed in us deserving to become "top of the line" in life. He continues to be worthy of treating himself to that level. Love you, Dad.

Prayerful thanks to Russ, the father of my daughters, who always hoped for an abundant life for us, with all good things. His wish for our success continues forward, and I remain so very grateful.

Thank you, thank you, thank you to the amazing groups of people (you know who you are) who encouraged me to extend my speaking talents and motivational insights to print. This book is for all of you!

Enthusiastic thanks to the awesome participants who attended my workshops entitled "Learning to Press Your Reset to Worthy Button" and "A Deeper Dive into Worthiness." Their positive feedback and insights both confirmed the relevance of my message and sparked the flame to encourage me.

Heartfelt thanks to all the mentors, spiritual guides, and educators who reminded me of the importance of hope, gratitude, and generosity. Through these graces, *It's Never Too Late to Be Worthy Of ...* blossomed. Many thanks to Weight Watchers for a career I have loved and am honored to have and for bringing the most amazing people to me, who have enriched my life.

Special thanks to my saints and angels, whose intercession on my behalf has led me through both joyous and difficult times. Sweet thanks to my Blessed Mother for her loving daily guidance and nurture, especially while writing this book. Blessed gratitude to God for His tender mercy throughout my life as well as for being my spiritual guide in the creation of my work and the delivery of my message to the world.